T0146601

# The AntiCAT Book

# The AntiCAT Book

## Why We Loathe and Abhor CATS
## Why We Love and Adore DOGS

# BRUCE SHEIMAN

# THE ANTICAT BOOK
## WHY WE LOATHE AND ABHOR CATS
## WHY WE LOVE AND ADORE DOGS

iUniverse books may be ordered through booksellers or by contacting:

iUniverse
1663 Liberty Drive
Bloomington, IN 47403
www.iuniverse.com
1-800-Authors (1-800-288-4677)

ISBN: 978-1-5320-3537-1 (sc)
ISBN: 978-1-5320-3536-4 (e)

Library of Congress Control Number: 2017918474

Print information available on the last page.

iUniverse rev. date: 01/19/2018

# Important Qualifying Note: Do Not Harm Any Living Creature

Please recognize that this book is *satire* and in truth I would never harm a cat. Nor do I endorse the physical or psychological abuse of any living creature for any reason.

Cat owners may claim that felines stand at the pinnacle of the animal kingdom, but in actuality that distinction belongs to humans. And as ethical beings it is our responsibility to treat all animals with kindness.

# Contents

**Introduction**
Cats Are Not Great: How Felines Ruin Everything .......... ix

**Chapter 1**
Fifteen Exquisite Reasons to Despise Cats ......................... 1

**Chapter 2**
Positive Proof Dogs Are Superior to Cats ........................ 27

**Chapter 3**
The Psychology of Cat People ......................................... 45

**Chapter 4**
The Feline Personality Exposed: What Cat People
Won't Tell You ............................................................... 63

**Chapter 5**
Indisputable Evidence: Dogs Are America's Favorite Pet .. 79

**Appendix**
The Great American Pet Competition:
An Exclusive Pet Preference Survey ................................. 87

# Introduction

# Cats Are Not Great:
# How Felines Ruin Everything

# Presenting a Contrarian Perspective

The pet world is divided into two groups – "dog people" and "cat people" – each claiming that its preferred animal is the reigning champion.

This dog-cat rivalry is one of the longest-running feuds in American culture – right up there with the New York Yankees and Boston Red Sox, Blue States and Red States, Coke and Pepsi, Microsoft and Apple.

*The AntiCAT Book* presents a contrarian perspective to all the syrupy-sweet volumes that portray cats as cuddly creatures and, instead, reveals cats to be what they really are: not-very-bright, difficult-to-train, self-centered animals that luxuriate in human benevolence but give little in return.

In the end, this book is a warning about the costs associated with bringing a cat into your home. Cat owners must come to terms with such offensive feline traits as odiferous litter boxes, regurgitated hairballs, screeching mating calls, an irrepressible killer instinct, destroyed personal property, pre-dawn wake-up visits, and fastidious dietary regimens.

In essence, the life of a cat has just three imperatives: energy input ("feed me"), waste output ("clean up my mess") and, in between, napping ("leave me alone").

# Dogs Play While Cats Prey

No species has developed a closer relationship with humanity than canines. Scientists now believe that this distinctive connection goes back 25,000 years, as humans and proto-dogs evolved together in an intimate symbiosis – a mutually beneficial relationship. In fact, dogs have remarkable mental and social skills that uniquely enable them to thrive in a human environment.

This book offers proof that, in the endless rivalry between canines and felines, dogs are eminently superior with respect to their cognitive skills, emotional intelligence, language comprehension, and service to humanity – all the while helping to make us better human beings.

This book also illuminates the profound *ethical* distinctions implied in feline and canine behavior. Just imagine your child adopting a cat's "philosophy of life" as opposed to a dog's. For example:

> ➤ Your dog brings you a Frisbee; your cat brings you a dead mouse.

> ➤ Your dog licks your face to express affection; your cat "sprays" your house to assert possession.

> ➤ Your dog plays using his paws; your cat preys using his claws.

> ➤ If animals could read, your dog would be curled up with Dale Carnegie's *How to Win Friends*, while your cat would be furtively studying Machiavelli's *The Prince*.

> ➤ If animals could speak, your dog's admiration would go to philanthropists like Bill Gates and Albert Schweitzer, while your cat's preferred role models would include Bernie Madoff and Jeffrey Dahmer.

# Illuminating Cats' True Nature

In effect, dogs live by the Golden Rule: treating others the way we all expect to be treated. Yet cats seem driven by the opposite principle: treating others as a means to get what they want.

Dogs have been bred over thousands of years to favor genes whose counterparts in humans select for exceptional friendliness. In the case of felines, it would seem that evolution has emphasized a misanthropic gene, in both cats and their humans – aptly expressed by one cat owner, "Frankly, the more people I meet in life, the more I love my three cats." Perhaps that's why dogs always seem to smile at people while cats are content to wear a persistent "sour puss."

Living with a cat may cultivate praise-worthy traits in its owner such as kindness, patience and humility. This book's foremost lesson, however, is that cats are anything but angelic animals.

While dogs' "wild wolf" brain was long ago bred out of existence, the common household feline has retained its wild cat brain, with deleterious consequences. Invariably, cats' cuteness belies their true nature as solitary hunters that cannot resist the temptation, even with full stomachs, to pounce on the most vulnerable creatures – perhaps a child's pet rabbit or a fledgling Blue Jay waiting for its mother to feed it.

In the end, this book offers a much-needed antidote to the deluge of cat-worship hyperbole we constantly hear from feline loyalists, such as: "Dogs believe they are human; cats believe they are God."

Regarding a cat's purported divinity, *The AntiCAT Book* explains why we should all take after Christopher Hitchens and Richard Dawkins and apply an unrelenting, unsparing skepticism.

# If Dogs and Cats Were People

This is the first book to articulate the differences between dogs and cats as we evaluate the other companions in our lives – in *human* terms.

Certainly we already do this in our pop-culture depictions of dogs and cats. And this is also what we do when we bring a pet into our lives. Ultimately, we are not adapting ourselves to the feline world or the canine world; rather, we are imposing our expectations on the pet.

And when I do that, having lived with both dogs and cats, I derive the observations that make up this book (with the addition of humor for entertainment value). Throughout this book, I strive to answer the questions: What kind of *people* are dogs and cats? What is their character, personality, temperament, style of living, and ethical orientation?

The following pages express my interpretations of the inner nature of dogs and cats. And at the end of this book, using the accompanying "Pet Preference Survey," you have the opportunity to convey *your* understanding of the differences between canines and felines.

# Fifteen Exquisite Reasons to Despise Cats

# Dare to Speak the Truth

Cohabitating with a cat may be the most lop-sided Darwinian arrangement in history. While dogs are universally beloved pets, cats are highly polarizing. Research has shown that more people love dogs than cats; yet more people dislike cats than dogs.

What cat owners fail to realize is that a cat's normal behavior positively begs for parody. Yet cat devotees continue to boast that their pets are transcendent beings in possession of great wisdom and mystical powers.

If cat owners knew the truth about their pets, I dare say there would not be a need for this book.

I feel like Copernicus telling his brethren that the universe does not revolve around the Earth. The time has come to push felines off their lofty pedestal.

What follows are my 15 reasons to loathe (not love) and abhor (not adore) cats.

# Reason No. 1
# Because Cats Are Not as Dumb as You Think – They're Dumber

The very definition of intelligence is the capacity to learn. But cats do not seem to learn much of anything. One recent news story revealed just how clueless cats can be.

A calico cat named Willow disappeared from its home in Colorado, only to be found on a Manhattan street five years later. Cat enthusiasts may claim that Willow is indeed a smart kitty, having survived all those years.

But I see circumstances differently. It would be one thing if Willow had spent that time battling against nature, like Lassie, to make its way back home. Instead, Willow traveled 1,800 miles *away* from its home.

And to witness a cat's obtuse nature firsthand, you need only to observe a house cat as it stares intently at a bird through a window. Then watch the cat leap for the bird and hit its head against the pane of glass, neglecting – for the umpteenth time – that the window is sealed shut.

These experiences suggest a clear lesson: Anyone who believes in "intelligent design" as a way to explain complex life forms has never known a cat.

# Reason No. 2
# Because Cats Are Not Dogs

We have all heard the same story from cat owners: They would never exchange their kitty for a puppy. But lurking in their subconscious is their true desire – they really do want a dog.

I have many first-person accounts where cat owners say their cats … kind of … behave like dogs (by which they mean equaling a dog's sweetness, playfulness and smarts).

This self-deception is similar to what is called anthropomorphism when we attribute human qualities to non-human objects.

When cat owners say their pet is capable of many dog-like behaviors, that is what I call *canine*pomorphism: They see Dog when they are really looking at Cat.

Let's face facts. Dogs have a cold nose but a warm heart. Cats have warm fur but a cold soul. Or as one friend put it, "I like animals that like me back."

Maybe in time pet medicine can offer these people a species-change operation. Until then, cat owners must move beyond their pooch envy.

# Reason No. 3
# Because Cats Clean Themselves with Their Own Saliva

Talk to cat owners and they will undoubtedly boast that cats have a built-in self-cleaning capacity. That intrinsic ability, however, relies on a mouth full of cat saliva. Does this make you want to be closer to cats? Given where that tongue has been, I want to be as far away as possible.

One of the harsher realities cat lovers need to acknowledge is that cats always clean themselves after they have been caressed by a "filthy" human.

# Reason No. 4
# Because Cats Are Cowards

Have you ever wondered where the expression "scaredy cat" comes from? Have you ever thought why you have never heard of a "watch cat"? In fact, the moment a stranger enters your home, the pusillanimous pussy immediately runs under a bed or into a closet.

We have seen many U.S. presidents with their dogs, but where are the presidential cats? Probably hiding under a rug in the Lincoln Bedroom.

# Reason No. 5
# Because Cats Have Wimpy Names

Some of the most nauseating names for cats include Precious (yuk), Fluffy (blah), Tiffany (sigh), Peaches (oy), Angel (geez), and Princess (ugh). Their names might as well be Sissy or Wuss.

And the irony is that in most cases cats do not even respond to their names, so stupid are they.

My recommendation is to choose cat names limited to one syllable.

# Reason No. 6
# Because the Egyptians
# Worshipped Cats

What can I say? Not every historical development results in a quantum leap for humankind. History is fraught with examples of taking one step backwards for every two steps forward. And worshipping cats is one of the instances when history took a detour from reason and rationality.

Need I remind you that the ancient Egyptians bequeathed to us hieroglyphics, when a simple typewriter would have been sufficient.

# Reason No. 7
# Because Cats Are the Pet Version of a Sociopath

It is no revelation that cats' normal behavior precisely fits that of a sociopath. Cats are manipulative and narcissistic. The message they convey in their behavior is, "Screw you and all of God's creatures." Like the sociopaths they are, cats have no regard for the feelings of others. They are aloof and dispassionate in their relations with humans, whom they only reluctantly tolerate in their territory.

Remember that cats kill. And when cats play with their food, the problem is that the food may still be ambulatory.

# Reason No. 8
# Because Cats Have Destructive Paws

I may not have a home worthy of *Architectural Digest*, but I do like the stuff I have. Truth be told, I have lived with two felines for longer than I care to admit. The reason? It had to do with another human whose bad habits almost made me appreciate the cats. I said *almost*. But that is how I came to possess my PhD in cat behavior.

From experience I can tell you that cats jump and scamper on all surfaces, including those on which humans prepare their meals. Cats produce damage to furniture, cause expensive objects to topple, and shed itinerant hairs on the dinner table.

And they do so with the same paws that minutes ago were used to bury their waste.

# Reason No. 9
# Because Cat Nature Goes Against Human Nature

Cats are schizoid. For some period of time they are forced to be domestic home bodies. But cats actually desire to spend most of their day in the "wild" where they can be solitary stalkers. Going for a walk with a human has no appeal to cats. Being obedient and modeling human behavior has no meaning for felines.

The moment a cat owner opens the door to the outside world, the cat takes off without looking back. As the cat crosses the threshold between inside and outside, the domesticated feline brain is supplanted by a wild-cat brain. And the owner knows she may not see the cat again for weeks or months – or in the case of Willow described above, *years*.

Yet the last time I looked, people are social-oriented animals just like dogs; as a consequence, humans are inherently more capable of relating to sociable canines than to solitary felines.

Thus dog nature is eminently compatible with human nature; but that is not the case with cats, whose nature runs contrary to human predilections. Feline proclivities actually work against human inclinations, while dogs are called "best friends" for two valid reasons: they *like* people and they *are like* people.

# Reason No. 10
# Because Cats Are an Eco-Menace

Domestic cats emerged with humans mainly as a way to control rodent populations, and eventually evolved from pest controls to pets. But are cats now evolving from pets to pests?

As children we learned from cartoons that cats are hunters, with Sylvester the Cat always on the prowl for Tweety Bird. But cats' real-world impact is no laughing matter.

The unfortunate reality is that cats generally have little respect for life. As a consequence, cats are a burgeoning environmental hazard. The nation's 70 million free-ranging cats are the most abundant population of carnivores in North America.

According to the National Audubon Society, "Worldwide, cats are involved in the extinction of more bird species than any other factor, except habitat destruction." The Smithsonian Zoo's Migratory Bird Center placed the number of birds felled by felines at between 1.4 billion to 3.7 billion per year. In fact, for every cat in the wild, 200 birds are killed annually.

Cats further disturb the natural environment as they hunt squirrels, rabbits and other small mammals. The World Conservation Union lists domestic cats as one of the worst invasive species. Indeed, Australia has one of the world's highest rates of mammal extinctions – 29 such extinctions have been documented over the past two centuries, and feral cats are thought to be the culprits in 27 of those disappearances.

Without a doubt, cats are ecological disasters; they are the *anti-green pet*.

# Reason No. 11
# Because Cats are "Killing Machines"

In his book, *Cat Watching*, Desmond Morris calls cats "an efficient killing machine." This comes from an expert who presumably likes cats. But no matter how strong his feline affinity, there's no getting around the truth.

A cat scratches and destroys the fabric of your favorite chair – a process euphemistically called "stropping" – so as to sharpen its claws. According to Morris, cat owners who do not want their favorite chairs "stropped" may choose to have their cats declawed, but he calls this a "cruel practice." Morris asserts: "A cat without its claws is not a true cat."

So you are confronted with a stark choice – either you have a "true cat" or a true chair; you cannot have both.

But I digress.

After an initial pounce, the cat's prey is pinned down using those sharpened claws. Then the cat quickly bites down with its long teeth aimed at the nape of the neck. With a rapid juddering movement of the jaw, the cat inserts its fangs into the neck of its prey between the vertebrae to sever the spinal cord. This is the "killing bite" that immediately incapacitates the prey.

Angelic creatures, indeed!

# Reason No. 12
# Because Cats Are Wicked

Many people believe that cats are deep into Satanism. What other conclusion can be drawn from a cat's malicious and destructive nature? Indeed, cats have been linked to witchcraft for centuries. In the 14th century, for example, Pope Innocent VIII encouraged the destruction of cats in his attempt to eradicate the black arts.

And I fail to believe that an entire religion could have gotten this completely wrong.

# Reason No. 13
# Because Cat Owners Are Easily Swayed by Nonsense

For example, the notions of Carl Jung as applied to cats. Could someone please tell me the meaning of this contorted statement I derived randomly from a book about cat behavior?

> "The cat is a living, breathing role model of the perfect balance and harmony of both anima and animus, and of the balance between co-dependency and radical interdependence."

The bottom line: Cats may not benefit from a psychotherapist (you cannot shrink what is not there) but surely their owners would.

# Reason No. 14
# Because a Cat Will Eat Your Face

If this book leaves you with one unforgettable truth, it is that cats are carnivores. I am reminded of cats' predatory nature by a magazine advertisement I saw for cat food that proclaimed, "Inside every cat lives the spirit of the wild – and a love for meat."

The implication is that birds and squirrels are not the only threatened animals. Indeed, if a ravenous cat is locked inside your house and you happen to have a heart attack or meet with some other unkind fate, the cat eventually will eat your face. I heard that on a *Sex and the City* episode, so I know it's true.

It seems that cats give new meaning to the expression "saving face." And the face you save may be your own.

Thus if you happen to live with a cat, just make sure that, whatever happens to you, there is sufficient premium cat food readily available to satisfy your feline's natural appetites.

# Reason No. 15
# Because Cats Are High-Maintenance Pets

Finally I have the opportunity to challenge one of the cat world's most infamous pieces of propaganda. My clinical research proves that cats have one of the highest cost-benefit ratios in the pet universe. (My research will be published in the peer-reviewed scientific journal, *Archives of Petology*.)

Quite simply, when people say cats are "low maintenance," they are referring to the resources required to maintain the cat, not the resources to maintain the integrity of your home and belongings.

In addition to the feline destructive habits, we must factor in the huge investment of time and effort required to train a cat to perform even elementary behaviors, especially if the desired behavior runs counter to a cat's natural inertia.

The only true reason we can say cats are "low maintenance" compared to dogs is because they nap most of the day and require minimal effort to keep them entertained. The writer Doris Lessing aptly summed up this pooch-feline distinction: "Dogs have an energetic and physical life. Cats are perfectly happy never doing anything."

# Three Reasons I Like Cats

I know people reading this book will think that I am a demented cat hater with too much time on my hands. While I admit the latter is true, the former is an unqualified falsehood. In fact, in the spirit of fairness and balance, I want to reveal the three things that I actually *like* about cats.

**Fair and Balanced Opinion No. 1** Living in Manhattan, I have learned that house cats rarely venture outside of their owner's home. What that means is, since I would never contemplate a friendship with a cat owner, I do not have to encounter a flesh-and-blood feline more often than, say, once every Total Solar Eclipse.

**Fair and Balanced Opinion No. 2** A large number of people find cats repulsive. Thus felines can chase away unwanted friends or neighbors who may seek to manipulate you. The irony, of course, is that you still have a friend that wants to manipulate you – the cat.

**Fair and Balanced Opinion No. 3** Okay, so I was only able to come up with two reasons.

# Positive Proof Dogs Are
# Superior to Cats

# Cats Owners' Excuses

It's axiomatic that feline apologists object to any depiction that favors dogs over cats. Thus feline experts claim that "cats are every bit as expressive as dogs; you just have to know how to speak their language." But that's precisely the point: In the case of dogs, they understand *my language*. In fact, researchers have shown that when listening, dogs use brain regions analogous to those humans use to understand what other people are saying.

Feline communication is often mysterious, even to cat owners, who frequently ask: What is my cat saying when he rubs against me or brings me a mouse cadaver? If cats were truly articulate in human terms, cat owners would not need to consult cat psychics, among other questionable interpreters of feline intentions.

Cat defenders also say that felines are as trainable as dogs – it's just that cats have a limited desire to please their owners. In fact, cat apologists reach the pinnacle of absurdity when they suggest that cats are not dumb, they just *act* dumb, paradoxically suggesting that cats are actually quite smart. (I guess the same could be said of my pet rock.)

The truth is, cats have evolved within human society for 10,000 years, but have not adapted as well as dogs to the human environment, and they have not developed the ethical sensibility, communication skill and learning capability to make them trustworthy partners.

# Dogs Reciprocate;
# Cats Manipulate

Every dog owner knows that pooches have a keen sense of right and wrong. A dog that breaks the house rules is quick to seek forgiveness. Indeed, moral behaviors – including altruism, tolerance, and fairness – are readily apparent in the egalitarian way dogs play with each other and with their human companions. Investigators at the Messerli Research Institute in Vienna have shown that dogs behave pro-socially, such as making an effort to help another dog even when there is no reward in it for them.

Cats, on the other hand, are known to be ruthless predators of smallish animals, which they kill instinctively. If cats can be considered "smart," it is usually a reference to their cunning and connivance in the natural selection process. This is the singular feline skill that is unrivaled among domestic animals.

One such cat, according to its owner, "was a good problem-solver, taking the bread we put out for the birds, placing it near a bush and laying in wait."

Revealingly, cat owners do not seem at all distressed that their pets' foremost skills pertain to killing. In this context, I am reminded of a *New Yorker* cartoon in which a cat with a handgun is shown aggressively shooting a bird to death; the caption reads: "What the hell was I *supposed* to do? I've been declawed!"

To understand the existential difference between cats and dogs, one need look no further than to two sets of fictional characters: Morris the Cat and Garfield (manipulative, exploitive) compared to Lassie and Benji (always helping someone).

# Dogs Have Heightened Emotional and Cognitive Skills

According to psychologist Erich Fromm, humans are motivated by *biophilia* – the need to be surrounded by a world that is fully "alive." Thus we love nature and seek to cohabitate with living beings that emotionally give back to us. And in the words of philosopher Martin Buber, humans seek an "I-Thou" relationship with living beings that respect our dignity and respond to our emotional needs.

In the case of either Fromm's biophilia or Buber's I-Thou relationship, dogs are far superior to cats. Dogs have a remarkable ability to grasp an extensive human vocabulary as well as nonverbal behavior.

Dogs are especially adept at cognitive tasks that require cooperation and sharing information to achieve a goal. Barking, for example, is rare in wild canines, suggesting it evolved to enable dogs to communicate with people.

Researchers are learning that, in many ways, dogs exhibit cognitive skills equivalent to those of a young child, which includes abilities scientists call "referential communication" (understanding images and pictures), "pedagogy" (exactly imitating a behavior shown by others) and "theory of mind" (deciphering the desires and intentions of people).

Dogs are like us in their joy, empathy and social affinity. It is no wonder that many canine devotees swear they have a bond with their dog approaching what they have with a friend. In fact, dogs are almost Christ-like: No matter how unworthy you are, they love you.

# Dogs' Humanitarian Role

In Western culture, dogs are virtually synonymous with heroism, nobility and loyalty. Humanitarian services performed by dogs include helping the blind and infirm, sniffing out bombs in Afghanistan, locating lost people, finding drugs on the Mexican border, and discovering cancer in patients. Indeed, of the 80 members of the commando team that flew to Abbottabad, Pakistan, and killed Osama bin Laden, one in particular had four legs.

Dogs also help the autistic. Autism impairs communication and the ability to form social bonds. According to Autism Service Dogs of America, while many children with autism cannot relate well to people, they can more easily relate to a dog. The bond with a dog bypasses the verbal dimension and goes straight to the emotional side of an autistic patient.

The variety of life-enhancing endeavors assigned to dogs is truly astounding. As one of many examples, psychiatric service dogs are specially trained to assist traumatized veterans reintegrate into society. These dogs help to speed recovery from the psychological wounds of war, resulting in drastic reductions in stress-disorder symptoms. In one clinical situation, just weeks after an Iraq war veteran got a dog, he was able to cut in half the dose of anxiety medications he took for post-traumatic stress disorder; further, this veteran's night terrors and suicidal thoughts came to an end.

Another noteworthy example is the case of a bloodhound from South Dakota named Calamity Jane. She helped recover dozens of missing people. When the dog eventually passed away, one admirer's condolence card read, "I have kept a scrap book on Calamity Jane's efforts and know that she will be long remembered for her service to mankind." That says it all.

# Dogs Are Faithful Companions

Almost everyone is familiar with the notion of "dog years," where we estimate a dog's age by equating its lifespan with that of a person. With no other species do we so intimately intertwine our lives. And no wonder: Dogs possess many of a human's most laudable attributes, while cats express some of the most lamentable. First and foremost, pets are meant to be companions. But I question whether domestic cats meet that definition beyond the wishful thinking of their owners.

Indeed, cats are more like elusive strangers than loyal friends. Imagine if you shared your living space with another person who rarely shows sincere acts of devotion, disappears for weeks at a time to have fun elsewhere, and destroys your personal possessions – would you consider that person a friend? Of course not.

When we lavish attention on dogs, we know that our affection is appreciated and rewarded. For example, dogs are the only animals that have learned to gaze directly into people's eyes as people gaze at each other.

In contrast, the life of a cat is deemed successful by the opposite measure: felines seem motivated to derive the greatest payoff from the *smallest* emotional investment. If cats are capable of complex behavior, it is almost entirely for their own machinations, not to please their human benefactors.

Thus, dogs and cats each have an acute sense of smell. In the case of dogs, it is used to discover bombs, narcotics, missing people, and cancer. In the case of cats, it's employed to locate the two-day-old tuna sandwich that dropped behind the couch.

# The Media Message:
# Dogs are Universally Loved

Remember that childhood game: If you could be any animal, what would it be? Well, if all of America were to choose an animal, most assuredly it would be a DOG. Thus it is no surprise that dogs are widely featured in the media.

We are all aware, of course, that dogs often share the limelight with humans as movie stars. Within a recent 12-month period, I viewed an astonishing nine movies on cable television where dogs played the featured role: *Hotel for Dogs, Adventures of Yellow Dog, Marley & Me, 101 Dalmatians, Good Boy!, Zeus and Roxanne, Beethoven, Must Love Dogs,* and *Underdog.*

In addition, I performed an informal survey of print ads and counted over 30 brands that show dogs as warm and friendly companions, including American Express, British Airways, CitiBank, Ford, General Motors, MasterCard, Quaker Oats, Ralph Lauren, Target Stores, and Xerox.

And what is the number of comparable ads that feature cute and cuddly cats? None, zero, nada – unless you count ads for allergy remedies and pet food.

The overwhelming prevalence of dogs rather than cats in the media is no mystery. Dogs are viewed as emotional peers to humans, whereas cats are understood to be hopelessly indifferent to human concerns.

# After the Break-Up:
# The Dog Is Little Different
# from a Child

Dogs are not mere possessions, like cats. It seems when a couple breaks up, who gets the cat is more like an ambivalent conundrum, easily resolved when one party says to the other: "Please take the cat since he belonged to you before the relationship's inception."

In the case of my former girlfriend, Cheri, she came with an adorable Chihuahua named Gizmo. Cheri had Gizmo for a full seven years before she knew me, so the reasonable expectation in the event of a break-up was that Gizmo would go with Cheri.

In the year before our break-up, however, Gizmo was fatally hit by a car in upstate New York. But within three months of our loss, we acquired Gracie, an almost exact replica of Gizmo. Most mysteriously, Gizmo's death and Gracie's birth occurred about the same time, in early September 2010.

The coincidence of their death-birth and their similar appearance made it seem that Gracie was more than just a pet replacement for Gizmo, but her "spiritual" replacement, which made her all the more special.

# The Similarities between Companions: Human and Canine

Cheri used to complain that Gracie brought me miles of smiles in a way that she herself never did. But that's the nature of a dog's love and enthusiasm. Plus, in the beginning Gracie did not exhibit any clear preference for Cheri, which she took too much to heart.

Cheri thought I was trying to steal her new dog's affections from her – and it is true that if Cheri entered this relationship with anything of her own, most certainly it was Gizmo. But Gracie was different. We chose that puppy together, when she was all of two months old and one-pound in weight. Gracie at this point belonged to both of us.

When Cheri moved out, a heart-wrenching experience under any condition, it was made all the harder because of my affections for Gracie. If she was not Gizmo's reincarnated replacement, Gracie was certainly her emotional substitute. The role Gracie played was much like the role of any child in a relationship.

# The Psychology of Cat People

# When Cat Vices Become Virtues

We know that cats are inscrutable, but what about cat owners – the people who seem unperturbed to accommodate an animal that appreciates so little?

Cat therapists (yes, there is such a profession) exist more for the cat owner than for the cat. Possibly that is because in the tug-of-war between cat and human, the cat is incapable of altering its behavior. The shrink is necessary to help the cat owner come to terms with the unchangeable nature of cat behavior.

This exasperating scenario leads to one conclusion: Rather than changing cat behavior, it is far easier to change people's *perceptions* of cat behavior.

In other words, a resolution is achieved when the cat owner chooses *to make a virtue of the problematic cat behavior.* Thus, in the cat owner's mind, a feline's predatory nature, destructive tendencies, and lack of empathy essentially become *admirable* traits. So don't be nonplussed when undisciplined cats are called "curious." Anti-social cats are labeled "independent." Selfish cats are claimed to be "self-sufficient." And so on.

This remarkable act of self-deception is likened to the Stockholm syndrome: the psychological condition where hostages (in this case humans) counter-intuitively exhibit positive feelings towards their captors (in this case cats).

# Are Cat Owners Masochists?

The single most common characterization of cats, even among those who adore felines, is their unqualified selfishness. Cat owners not only seem to indulge a cat's natural self-centeredness; they appear to relish a cat's outright rejection. Cat apologists go out of their way to boast about the disdain cats have for them, and astonishingly they are proud of it.

Cat lovers also take delight in claiming that *they* are owned by their cats, not the other way around. All this cat adulation begs the question: How is it that cat enthusiasts so easily acquiesce to feline dominance?

Simply, cat devotees feel they are truly in the presence of a superior being. After all, if the cat is capable of manipulating humans to get everything they want without offering much in return, then *they must be superior*, or so goes cat apologists' bewildering logic.

We have all witnessed this kind of self-depreciation before. When devotion to another being becomes overwhelmingly one-sided, *masochism* naturally springs to mind.

What other possible explanation is there for a cat lover's predictable reaction ("That's so adorable!") to a cat swallowing a former member of an endangered avian species or a cat wearing a Gestapo costume?

# A Cat's Guide to Mastering Humans

As if to emphasize a cat's dominant position, cat owners have been known to engage in a perplexing role reversal – making believe they are "cats" giving advice to other "cats" about how to manipulate their human servants.

In one such scenario, a "cat" advises: "Sometimes, despite your best training efforts, your human will stubbornly resist bending to your will. In these cases, you may have to punish your human." Two obvious punishment options are offered:

> ➤ "If you have to vomit, make sure it is in a spot that a bipedal human is likely to step on."

> ➤ "When marking your territory [spraying or urinating], make sure it is in a place that your human *must* notice, such as the middle of the bed."

On other matters of feline power politics I derived from cat websites:

> ➤ "It is important to maintain your dignity when around humans so that they will not forget who is the master of the house."

> ➤ "Humans often assume they have higher priorities than taking care of a cat's needs. By pestering your human when she is most busy, she will undoubtedly give you anything you want."

These quotations make it very clear that cat owners envision felines as their bosses and not the other way around; humans are mere supplicants in the service of their feline superiors.

# It's a Cat-Eat-Bird World

Remarkably, cat enthusiasts boast about the unbalanced power arrangement that prevails between felines and humans. As a result, cat owners happily articulate such aphorisms as: "In a cat's eye, all things belong to cats"; "To keep a true perspective of one's importance, everyone should have a dog to worship him and a cat to ignore him"; and "Dogs look up to you; cats look down on you."

I guess this teaches humans humility. All of which suggests the question: What if the world were governed by a cat's rules of life? And you thought a dog-eat-dog world is cruel. Perhaps we need to change that expression to a *cat-eat-bird world* when describing the harshness of life.

What a group of dogs want is social order and a clear leader. Cats want their own territory with no other *living* creature in it – dead animals, however, are okay as illustrated by a cat named Snuggles.

It seemed that Snuggles had a routine of bringing home dead mice and birds clenched in his jaw. But there was a concern. The owner could not find a trace of these dead animals, so she assumed the cat ate them whole. Weeks later, the stench of rotting flesh permeated the house. It seems that Snuggles did not eat all the creatures it killed, but stashed their remains in the guest bedroom.

And the irony is the sweet-sounding names given many cats as if to disguise their predatory nature. In the case described above, "Snuggles" is a real misnomer.

# Dog and Cat Owners' Psychological Differences

It is often said that people look like their pets. I am not sure that is true, but I have no doubt that people share their pet's temperament. Thus, if dogs and cats are substantially different, it makes sense that dog and cat owners exhibit parallel differences in character and personality.

Proof comes from a survey performed by a University of Texas psychologist measuring dog lovers and cat lovers on the basis of five major personality traits: extroversion, agreeableness, conscientiousness, neuroticism, and openness. The psychologist discovered that:

A full 46% of respondents described themselves as dog people, while just 12% said they were cat people; the remainder said they were both or neither.

> ➤ According to the psychologist, dog people are generally more friendly and personable; specifically, they are 15% more extroverted than cat people, 13% more agreeable, and 11% more conscientious.

> ➤ Cat people were generally 12% more neurotic than dog people and 11% more open.

These findings invariably lead to the question: Who would you rather be friends with – an extroverted, agreeable and conscientious dog person or an open but neurotic cat person?

# Do "Real Men" Live with Cats?

As more men are comfortable cohabitating with cats, they are acquiescing to the same subterfuge of making feline liabilities into virtues. One male cat owner, clearly wanting to dispel the stereotype that men who own cats are gay, had this to say:

> "Dogs are for the weakest of spirit. If you're feeling insecure about your place in the world, you get a dog because he will always back you up. A dog is an insecure man's best friend. And a man with a cat is secure with himself. After all, he's sharing his space with a predator."

I do not understand why anyone would choose to share his space with a predator, but I guess this proves that "real men" live with cats.

The reality, however, is quite different. In my commonsense view, cats are for submissive and weak-willed men (echoing the party line that cats dominate the relationship) and dogs are for mature, confident men who want in their pet a true companion.

Moreover, if I were a single woman in search of a loving man, I would immediately question the relationship potential of a guy who chooses to live with an emotionally distant animal – it could be a sign he has an intimacy disorder.

# Making Lemonade

In an endeavor worthy of Sisyphus, cat apologists struggle to give felines a favorable public identity. In particular, when comparing felines to canines, cat loyalists are prepared to stretch logic almost to the breaking point. For example:

> We know that dogs need to be walked outside their owner's home, whereas cats do their waste disposal inside. Besides the obvious advantage of getting the dog to do its dirty work outside, there are many ancillary benefits to walking a dog – from socializing with passersby to cardiovascular exercise to just getting out and about.

But leave it to a cat apologist to find the potential catastrophe in dog walking, no matter how unlikely: "Walking a dog can kill you," writes one cat proponent, "either through an accident, exposure to the elements or attacks by other animals. But I doubt that stroking a purring cat has ever resulted in a single death."

That someone can actually consider dog walking a risky behavior on par with going to war or working in a coal mine leaves me almost speechless.

I suggest that cat owners and their allies read the last section of this chapter for additional perspective.

# Maybe Cat People Really Are Crazy

Can there be a plausible explanation for cat apologists' loopy logic and nutty notions? A recent report in *New Scientist* magazine suggests there is.

The parasite *Taxoplasma gondii*, related to the bug that causes malaria, has been associated with such ailments as schizophrenia and obsessive-compulsive disorder, and is transmitted to humans via the predator-prey relationship between cats and mice.

In a cat, *Taxoplasma* resides in the wall of the small intestine and passes out through its waste. Once excreted, the parasite is picked up by rodents and other animals, forming cysts in brain, liver and muscle tissue. Eventually, if the parasite's rodent host is eaten by a cat, the infection cycle begins anew.

In susceptible humans, the parasite interferes with the brain's dopamine system, and is implicated in mental illness – specifically, schizophrenia and neuroticism. Thus cats pose a health risk to people with weakened immune systems.

This realization should also make cat owners think twice about locating the litter box in any household space related to personal hygiene, such as a bathroom, kitchen or bedroom.

Experts say that the best defense is to avoid contact with cat litter and cat droppings. In other words, don't own a cat.

# The Feline Personality Exposed: What Cat People Won't Tell You

# Who Owns Whom?
# You Are Part of a Cat's Territory

Cats may not like to be touched by people, including their owners, but they do not always accord humans the same deference, with some unappealing consequences.

Cats have scent glands near the anus that secrete a foul-smelling, urine-soaked substance as a means of marking territory and warding off predators. Among their "scented" possessions, cats include their owner and their owner's home. Thus, when a cat rubs against you, he is not necessarily being friendly; he is claiming you as part of his territory.

Feline apologists often claim that cats are vigilant, just like dogs, and seek to protect their owners from home incursions. Let me point out the relevant distinction here: In the case of dogs, they are protecting their *companions*; in the case of cats, they are protecting their *property*.

In any event, I would hate to live in a household in which many cats fuss over their human "possessions."

# Cats' Top Priority

A cat's restricted behavioral repertoire and limited communications capacity are evidenced by a number of rituals that cat owners must decipher every day.

Fortunately, most cat behaviors generally convey the same message, as indicated by the chart of the following page.

| Cat Behavior | Translation |
|---|---|
| Cat wakes you in the morning | "You were expecting maybe a rooster? Don't be silly: I ate it. And I'm still famished." |
| Cat welcomes you in the evening | "You're late. And I hope that take-out food is for *moi*." |
| Cat purrs and caresses you | "Don't flatter yourself. I'm hungry again." |
| Cat ignores favorite chicken dish | "B-o-r-i-n-g. I had this yesterday." |
| Cat naps | Dream imagery: feasting. |
| Cat emerges from slumber | "Drat: only a dream. Feed me now!" |

# The Myth of a Cat's Mind

One cat owner boasted that cats are smarter than dogs because her weeks-old kitten "knew" what to do when placed in a litter box but her puppy in the same situation was clueless. And another cat proponent asked, "Which animal would survive the longest if evicted from the house?"

The implication is that a dog's dependence on humans would be a disadvantage in the survival sweepstakes, but that cats' self-sufficiency would more likely result in greater longevity; hence, cats must be smarter, right?

Wrong. The behavior cited above is *instinct*, not *intelligence* which I define as the capacity to learn. Many dog behaviors are in fact learned. Indeed, our own flesh-and-blood children similarly pop out of the womb with few genetic instructions – it is proof of higher mammals' reliance on learning.

Ample evidence backs up these claims. For instance, researchers at CanCog Technologies, an institute that studies animal behavior, tested dogs and cats. They concluded that cats make more errors and require more trials to learn the same tasks as dogs.

I understand that cat owners assert that felines "have a mind of their own" to explain their inability to follow directions, but in actuality cat behavior has little to do with "minds."

# You Can Teach a Cat Anything – If You Have Nine Lifetimes to Accomplish It

Aren't euphemisms wonderful? They can make an intolerable situation almost endurable. Euphemisms abound when you live with cats. Take the "litter box." It brings to mind a receptacle for discarded paper and other dry household detritus. Instead, it is an effort to sugarcoat the potent stench of a cat's waste. Invariably, the cat traipses through the house with paws coated in litter dust as well as remnants of last night's savory salmon dinner.

Cat enthusiasts, of course, have the perfect solution to this problem: toilet train the cat. Here is step-by-step what you must do when attempting (success is not guaranteed) to toilet train your cat:

(1) First, you must move the litter box from its current location to the bathroom in small, slow steps. If the box is in the kitchen or basement, this process alone can take weeks.

(2) Once the cat is accustomed to the box's new location in the bathroom, elevate the litter box a little bit every few days or weeks until it is level with the toilet seat. To accomplish this, one cat owner suggested using a growing tower of pizza boxes affixed to the floor with duct tape.

## Not Finished Yet

Believe it or not, despite the weeks or months of tedium you have endured to this point, you have not reached the most difficult part.

(3) Once the cat is jumping up to his elevated litter box, you must transition the box into the toilet and gradually make the cat comfortable with water in the toilet. This challenge may require a Master's Degree in mechanical engineering. One cat trainer suggests using an aluminum roasting pan filled with a couple of inches of water that fits inside the toilet bowl.

(4) As the cat is habituated to reaching the toilet seat, you begin cutting a hole in the pan, widening it over time so that the toilet water eventually takes the place of the cat litter.

On average the entire toilet-training process might take a year. That's right – 12 months. And while that may not be quite nine lifetimes, it will surely feel like it.

## Managing the Downside Risks

Moreover, the process is not always successful. In one instance, a woman attempted to train her cat but the animal did not take well to the exercise and protested by going to the bathroom all over the house. In another case, a cat fell into the toilet, freaking out the animal to the point where the entire enterprise had to be abandoned.

One problem I see with this arrangement pertains to guests, who may not find sharing a bathroom with a cat very sanitary. Just imagine this scenario: At a friend's party you're waiting to use the bathroom, thinking all along it is occupied by another guest. Then, finally, the door is whisked open and out walks … a cat.

Assuming, however, the bathroom training *is* successful, we're never told if the cat is also taught to flush the toilet. If not, that last act of indignation is yours alone.

# B.F. Skinner to the Rescue

Among the tasks to teach a cat, using the toilet has to be among the most challenging. But training a cat to perform even simple behaviors can be exasperating. While cat owners never cease telling everyone that cats are quick learners, feline laziness and stubbornness are widely acknowledged throughout the pet world.

Dozens of books address cat behavior, and their message is the same: Cats are near impossible to train. The following reference was derived from the sales spiel for a book about cat behavior: "Perhaps you think training a cat is an impossible task. Maybe you think your cat is too independent. Outwitting a cat means persuading him that what you want is what he wants."

Intriguingly, these books make it sound as if you're teaching cats brain surgery, when the emphasis is usually on simple behaviors the average puppy routinely learns in a few weeks.

Another book tells cat owners not to expect feline learning to go much beyond simple conditioned response: "What's that you say? It's impossible to train a cat? You may not realize that you've already been training your feline. Does your cat rush to the kitchen every time you use the can opener? Does your cat perk up every time you pull out the grooming comb? These behaviors are proof your cat can be trained."

No doubt Pavlov and Skinner would be impressed with these examples of behavioral conditioning, but not the typical dog owner.

# Why Are Cats So Similar?

The fact that cats cannot easily be taught elementary behaviors, and then only with a great expenditure of time and effort, explains a phenomenon that perplexes most pet owners: Why are dogs so diverse but cats so much alike?

Dogs come in a wide variety of shapes, sizes and temperaments, mainly because humans have long cultivated canines to assist with particular tasks, such as hunting, guiding the blind or pulling a sled. By comparison, domesticated cats are largely homogeneous, differing mainly in the characteristics of their coats.

The reason: Felines have been largely useless to humans. Compared to canines, cats' unwillingness or inability to perform a number of tasks useful to humans has resulted in minimal selective breeding.

Thus the value of cats to people has not evolved much beyond rodent control and youthful cuteness – and the latter for just a brief time; the problem with kittens is that they inevitably grow up to be cats.

With regard to domesticated cats, therefore, it seems that one size and shape fits all.

# Further Reading

Should you choose to live with a cat despite my protests, I promise not to gloat or offer the clichéd "I told you so."

In fact, with the aim of easing the transition to a feline-dominated household, I recommend the following literary classics to help you better understand the predictable challenges in the relationship between felines and their human sugar daddies.

| | |
|---|---|
| *Of Human Bondage* | *Dangerous Liaisons* |
| *Lord of the Flies* | *To Kill a Mockingbird* |
| *Paradise Lost* | *A Comedy of Errors* |
| *The Waste Land* | *Loves Labor Lost* |
| *The Descent of Man* | *Les Miserables* |

# Indisputable Evidence: Dogs Are America's Favorite Pet

# The Journey Is Almost Over

Surely I know that dogs come with their own liabilities. Dogs do a number of annoying things: they drool, hump your leg, have bladder accidents, and bark loudly.

Despite a modest downside profile, however, dogs are without a doubt America's favorite pet. And while cats are highly revered, they are also widely reviled.

In fact, Americans say they dislike cats more than any other pet, with the exception of snakes and spiders. That's right – the only "pets" people dislike more than furry, fluffy cats are slimy, slivery things and creepy, crawly things.

Cat proponents' major defense to the criticism leveled against their petulant pets is the fact that there are more cats in American homes than dogs, which in their minds make cats the true champions. Forget about surveys that suggest cats rank low on the pet-likeability scale, they say, because cats win where it counts – in numbers.

According to the American Pet Products Association and the ASPCA, there are 78 million pet dogs in America and 85.8 million pet cats. This is the great "aha" moment for cat owners in their timeless rivalry with dog lovers. But in no way do these figures tell the whole story. Cat owners should not break out the celebratory sirloin (for the cat; the human will eat a burger) just yet.

# Dog Homes Outnumber Cat Homes

Rather than the absolute number of pet cats in American homes, the more meaningful statistic is the number of cat households compared to dog households. It seems that the average cat-owning home is occupied by 2.14 felines and the average dog-owning home has 1.54 canines.

Doing the math, we discover there are 50.6 million dog-owning households in the U.S. compared to 40.25 million cat-owning homes. This makes dogs the more popular pet.

And I am convinced the number of cat households is maintained artificially high. I estimate that among people who own cats, as many as 20 percent would prefer a dog, but either they do not have the wherewithal (money, attentiveness and/or space) to do right by a dog or they live in apartments whose landlords do not allow dogs; thus, many of these people may opt for a cat instead.

And I believe this is the explanation for many cat owners' claims that their feline pets exhibit dog-like behaviors, what I previously called *canine*pomorphism – because they really do want a dog.

# Why Dogs Rule – The Value of Empathy

Scientists have discovered that dogs possess an uncanny ability to intuit what people are thinking and feeling – the result of dogs' sensitivity to human verbal and emotional communication.

Yet diehard cat people often disparage a dog's innate capacity for empathy as "excessive neediness." According to the most fervent cat enthusiasts, dogs do little more than "grovel" and "suck-up" to humans. Dogs constantly "crave attention," leading one cat owner to disdainfully assert: "If you desire a complete co-dependent, you get a dog."

In contrast to servile dogs, feline proponents boast that cats are superior by virtue of their independence and self-reliance, leading one cat apologist to ask, "Which human partner would you prefer to live with: one always in-your-face with giddy enthusiasm [*like a dog*] or one whose love and trust must be earned over time [*like a cat*]?"

I know the kind of companion I prefer. Indeed, I cannot imagine a relationship with another living being lacking in empathy or a partner who does not need me. That is why for me dogs easily win the "Great American Pet Competition."

*And on the following pages you now have the opportunity to vote for your favorite pet.*

# APPENDIX

# The Great American Pet Competition: An Exclusive Pet Preference Survey

# Join the Debate:
# Complete Our Pet Preference Survey

Which pet – dogs or cats – makes the best companion? Which pet – canines or felines – is more:

- ➤ Intelligent?
- ➤ Playful?
- ➤ Empathetic?
- ➤ Affectionate?
- ➤ Communicative?
- ➤ Enthusiastic?
- ➤ Loyal?
- ➤ *Human*?

You now have the opportunity to vote for your favorite pet. Whether you are a dog-person or cat-person, please fill out our exclusive Pet Preference Survey on our website: AntiCatBookSurvey.com

# Make Your Voice Heard

While *The AntiCAT Book* is satire, no doubt I have offended more than a few cat enthusiasts. The Pet Preference Survey gives you the opportunity to speak back.

I understand that many people are lovers of both dogs and cats. And the best pet ultimately is the one most suited for the individual. However, it is difficult to ignore the fact that most of us prefer one pet over the other. As a result, I expect this brief survey to elicit strong passions on both sides of the dog-cat divide.

By responding to the survey, you are participating in the most illuminating pet-opinion survey ever undertaken. We all like to think of our pets as "human." This is your chance to tell the world just how human.

# Go to *The AntiCAT Book* Website

The purpose of this survey is to capture the perspectives of cat lovers and dog lovers on many pet attributes. Significantly, this questionnaire asks you to evaluate *both dogs and cats* on the same attributes. That way, we will be able to measure how dog-people see their preferred pet as compared to cats, and how cat-people see their favored pet as compared to dogs.

Responses to this survey will be continually tabulated, with regular updates presented on the book's website: AntiCatBookSurvey.com

Thank you for taking the time to share your thoughts about the Great American Pet Competition. This is the only survey of its kind and your answers will be making history in the pet world.

*Please note that this survey is open to everyone; you do not have to currently own a pet to complete this survey.*

# The AntiCAT Book
# Pet Preference Survey

1.  Check the one choice that best describes you.

    Dog Person        / /
    Cat Person        / /
    Both              / /
    Neither           / /

2.  Please indicate whether you *currently* own dogs and/ or cats.

    Yes                No

3.  Please indicate *in the past* whether you or your household has owned dogs and/or cats.

    Yes                No

4.  If you replied "yes" to either or both questions No.2 and No. 3 above, in total how many dogs and/or cats have you and/or your immediate family owned?

    Dogs    1    2    3    4    5    6+

    Cats    1    2    3    4    5    6+

5. How do you see the differences between dogs and cats? On the chart below, please rate dogs *and* cats on a five-point scale for the identified attributes, where 5 is your highest rating and 1 is your lowest.

| DOGS | ATTRIBUTES | CATS |
|:---:|:---:|:---:|
| **Rating Cats and Dogs** 5 = Highest; 1 = Lowest | | |
| 1 2 3 4 5 | *Affectionate* | 1 2 3 4 5 |
| 1 2 3 4 5 | *Aggressive* | 1 2 3 4 5 |
| 1 2 3 4 5 | *Agreeable* | 1 2 3 4 5 |
| 1 2 3 4 5 | *Calming* | 1 2 3 4 5 |
| 1 2 3 4 5 | *Clean* | 1 2 3 4 5 |
| 1 2 3 4 5 | *Communicative* | 1 2 3 4 5 |
| 1 2 3 4 5 | *Destructive* | 1 2 3 4 5 |
| 1 2 3 4 5 | *Empathetic* | 1 2 3 4 5 |
| 1 2 3 4 5 | *Enthusiastic* | 1 2 3 4 5 |

## Differences between Cats and Dogs (continued)

| Rating Cats and Dogs 5 = Highest; 1 = Lowest | | |
|:---:|:---:|:---:|
| **DOGS** | **ATTRIBUTES** | **CATS** |
| 1 2 3 4 5 | *Independent* | 1 2 3 4 5 |
| 1 2 3 4 5 | *Intelligent* | 1 2 3 4 5 |
| 1 2 3 4 5 | *Loyal* | 1 2 3 4 5 |
| 1 2 3 4 5 | *Moral* | 1 2 3 4 5 |
| 1 2 3 4 5 | *Obedient* | 1 2 3 4 5 |
| 1 2 3 4 5 | *Playful* | 1 2 3 4 5 |
| 1 2 3 4 5 | *Predatory* | 1 2 3 4 5 |
| 1 2 3 4 5 | *Selfish* | 1 2 3 4 5 |
| 1 2 3 4 5 | *Trusting* | 1 2 3 4 5 |

Printed in the United States
By Bookmasters